Living through Your Divorce

Living through Your Divorce

Earl A. Grollman
Marjorie L. Sams

With photographs by Steve Weinrebe

BEACON PRESS   Boston

Copyright © 1978 by Earl A. Grollman and Marjorie L. Sams

Photographs copyright © 1978 by Beacon Press

Beacon Press books are published under the auspices
of the Unitarian Universalist Association

Published simultaneously in Canada by
Fitzhenry & Whiteside Ltd., Toronto

Printed in the United States of America

(hardcover)   9   8   7   6   5   4   3   2   1

Library of Congress Cataloging in Publication Data

Grollman, Earl A
   Living through your divorce.
    1.   Divorce—Handbooks, manuals, etc.   2.   Divorce—
Psychological aspects.   I. Sams, Marjorie L., joint
author.   II. Title.
HQ814.G87   301.42′84   77–22117
ISBN 0–8070–2730–8

Nothing can bring you peace but yourself.

Ralph Waldo Emerson
"Essay on Self Reliance"

Contents

What This Book Is About

Our book is dedicated to you—as you face one of the most difficult experiences of your life.

We do not present superficial reassurances and easy answers. Rather, we offer the comfort that comes from discovering that you are not alone in feeling anguish, that your pain is normal, and that this major life change can lead to a meaningful future.

We suggest that you read this book with pencil in hand. Enter into dialogue. Write on it. Cross out. Underline. Add your own words. Allow *Living Through Your Divorce* to be your friend to assist you in describing your feelings and help you with practical suggestions and insights.

A chapter in your life has ended.

A new chapter is about to be written.

The preface to your life is Now.

Living through Your Divorce

1 Separation

Separation

It's over.
You have taken the
   wedding ring off.
The marriage is finished.
Hopes, promises, dreams
   are unfulfilled.

How could this have happened?

You were in love,
you were loved.

"Marriage is a sacred institution."

You believed it.
You made a commitment.
You expected to be happy.

It didn't work out that way.
No storybook ending.
You didn't live happily ever after.

You walk past a mirror,
  see a face,
  turn back.

You look again,
  and see a stranger in pain.

"My God, is that me?"

You are unprepared for the change
  in your life.
When you fill out an application
for a new account, you write
  married.

Then you remember.

Quickly, you write
  divorced.

It hits you.

Divorce.

That word.
Doesn't it mean *failure*?
Will people pity your children
    because they are from a *broken* family?

Broken.

That's what you are.

Divorce is a kind of death.
In many ways it is worse.

With death, there is a funeral.
There are
    flowers,
    words of sympathy,
    hugs,
    talk of happy memories.
Friends and family come together.
They grieve with the survivor.

In divorce, one mourns alone.

For divorce there is no public ceremony.
No crowd of comforting friends.

There was just a day in court.
All business.
Legal jargon,
    lawyers,
        uninvolved strangers.

No comfort.
No sympathy.
No real feelings allowed.

You wanted to laugh or scream.

The marriage is dead,
But there is no corpse to mourn over.
The ex is out there somewhere.

There is unfinished business.

So much unfinished business.

The Futility of Speech

Everyone gives unsolicited
    advice:
        "Stay together."
        "Don't be a quitter."
        "You want too much out of life."
        "Think of the children."
        "Marriage means sacrifice."
        "Divorce is the easy way out."
        "You have to give at least
            eighty percent."
        "Be realistic."
        "Think of your future."

You are in pain,
and friends
talk in clichés.

Suggestions often come from
unhappily married couples.

Simply say, "Thanks for your
advice."
Then do what is best for you.
It's your decision,
your life.

So many words.
The two of you tried to talk it out,
  justify,
    explain,
      and find the right
        answers.

After a while, you can't figure
  out the right
    questions.

Words don't seem to make any sense.
Just the realities.

One of you has moved out.
The wedding ring is in a drawer.

In Search of Self

Who am I now?
I used to share my name,
    my identity.
What am I?

"I am divorced.
        Ex-partner,
            ex-lover,
                ex-husband,
                    ex-wife.

"I am a half person.
    I can't go on like this."

    Your world is a nightmare.

    You feel lost.

With good reason.

You may have lost a companion,
    helper around the house,
    co-parent,
    cook and laundress,
    carpenter and plumber,
    father-figure,
       or mother-figure.

There's more.
You may have lost a home,
    a town,
    a job,
    your church,
    a club,
    your crowd.

Your losses are many.

They are real.

The decision to break the marriage vow
    is as momentous
    as your decision to marry.

2 Grief

The Many Faces of Grief

You are going through a grieving
    process,
a natural response to
    separation.

Normal fear and anxiety are
    essential to the preservation of life.

They teach you caution—
    the yellow light between red
        and green.

Grief is one of the most basic of
    human emotions.

When you grieve,
   you may have many different
   feelings in the space of a few moments.

"I am so tired,
   so angry,
      so jealous,
         so depressed,

"so relieved."

   You may be calm one minute;
      in turmoil the next.

   Each person experiences emotions in a
      different way.

   Yet there are some points of reference.

   You may recognize some of them.

Denial

"This is just a bad dream.
   When I wake up, I'll find
      that it really didn't happen."

   Secretly, you think or pretend that
      you are still married.

"My ex will return,
      apologize and change,
      and want me back.
   Just wait and see."

   Life will go on as before.

Denial is natural because the two of you
  lived together so long.

You are unable to admit
  that the marriage has ended.
You are afraid of starting anew.

Disbelief is often temporary.

You may simply need time before you can
  admit the truth.

Numbness

You have no feelings left.
You yawn; you fidget.
You can't concentrate.

It's impossible to settle down.

You seem not to hear the voices around you.
The whole world is unreal.
You are drained.

It's hardly worth starting
    anything new.
Nothing is certain anymore.

You'll never be able to count on
    anyone,
        or anything again.

It's understandable.
The person and the dreams
    you believed in
    no longer exist.

You are stunned.
Your sensibilities are numbed.
It's even hard to breathe.

Anger

"I'm not perfect.
  But I tried;
  God knows how I tried.
  Why me?"

  You hate your ex;
    want revenge.

"My life is destroyed.
  I'll get even.
  Nobody does this to me and
    gets away with it.

"Nobody."

You find yourself becoming
    annoyed with your friends.
Didn't they know what was going on?
They should have helped.
Whose side are they on?

And your children.
If it weren't for them,
    you might have separated a long time ago.
After the divorce, you are still responsible
    for them.

Resentment is a normal part
of the separation process.

You will be angry as long as
you don't accept the change.

As your pain subsides,
so will your anger.

Jealousy

You can't help yourself.
You keep thinking,

"I wonder if my ex is
    missing me?
    wanting me?
    hating me?
    seeing someone?"

Your mind is tortured with
    fantasies of your ex
    having a ball without you.

And here you are
    alone
    and miserable.

Frankly, you are jealous
   of your ex, who may be
   doing well without you;

   of the good life you might
      have had together;

   of the married couples who
      seem so happy;

   of people who
      have all the luck.

Ambivalence

There are times when you wish
that you were back together again.
Maybe you wouldn't be in such pain.

At least you would have somebody
   around,
even to argue with,
to share the responsibilities.

Then there are times when you're glad
   the ordeal is over.

You've been tortured long enough.

Enough is enough.

One moment,
  you want the marriage resumed.
The next moment,
  you want the separation.

With divorce, thoughts are not
  consistent and reconcilable.

Nor are feelings or actions.

Panic

You may have
    frightening dreams . . .

of being smothered,
    of being lost,
        of falling
and knowing no one is there
    to hold you.

You find yourself doing crazy things.

Getting lost on a familiar street.
Lighting a cigarette
    and finding the last one is still burning.
Overreacting to strange noises at home.
Losing track of time.

Playing detective . . . spying on your ex.
Forgetting whether the red light
    means stop or go.
Picking up the phone and not
    knowing whom you can call.

Buying things, anything.
Panicking over things you used
    to do with confidence,
    like driving at night.

"Why can't I get hold of myself?
Other people have gone through divorce.
They seem to manage so well."

You are emotionally disorganized.

Fatigue

You are tired.

You collapse in bed; but you can't sleep.
When you finally fall asleep, you don't rest.
You awaken exhausted.
You lie there, hanging on to the
   pillow as long as possible.
No reason to get up.
Nothing to look forward to.

The slightest effort leaves you limp.

Physical Pain

Emotional suffering brings physical distress.

Your stomach feels queasy,
as if there is something ugly inside you.

Inside your chest you may feel a pain,
   as if a jagged rock pressed
   against your ribs.

You have little or no appetite.
You eat because you are expected to.
Food has no taste.
After the meal, you feel unsatisfied.

You may feel dizzy.
You may get rashes,
terrible headaches.
Your back is killing you.

The pain is not imagined.
It is real.
Grief does cause physical changes.

They are your body's response
    to mental anguish.

Guilt

"If only I had been
more understanding,
forgiving,
accepting."

"If only I had
done this,
not done that,
tried harder."

So many regrets.

You feel like a complete failure.

You have enough pain.

Blaming yourself is pointless.

You don't solve problems
  with "if only."

The past is over.

Depression

"Nobody wants me."
"Who could love me?"

You feel rejected,
    put aside,
    cast off,
    alone, naked, unprotected.

Time drags.
Days are long.
Nights are longer.
You find no pleasure in anything or anyone.

You are useless.
You are empty.

So is the world around you.

But what did you expect?
To fill the void immediately?
To go on living as before?

Divorce is unbearable sorrow
   and loneliness.

Grief is the result
   of severing part of your life,
   of having to face new decisions
      on your own.

3 Decisions

Legal Decisions

The proceedings are over.
You have had your day in court.

But your marriage ended a
    long time ago.

You know that.

Papers are officially signed.
The date marks the legal
end of a marriage.

Your "marital status" is changed.
The divorce is final.
You may feel relief.

But it's not really over.
There is still much to resolve.

You phone your lawyer.

Calls are not quickly answered.

He cannot see you immediately.

You are angry.

Lawyers are busy with many clients.

Their background is not in family counseling.

Make an appointment.

Prepare yourself for it.

You can help by being brief,

    frank,

    as organized as possible.

Whenever you talk to lawyers,

    their fee clock is running.

Decisions About Money

The whole business of the financial settlement
    makes you panic.
Never have you felt more intimidated.

You may think
    "I'm going to be taken to the cleaners."
    "I'll be back to where I was when I was
        first married."
    "I'm going to be stone-cold
        broke."
    "I'll never make it."
"Never."

When a pie is cut,

you have to make do with only a part.

There's no way around it.

Lifestyles are altered

    after a divorce settlement.

You may need to seek employment

    to make ends meet.

Or take another job to supplement your

    income.

It is especially difficult if you

    never handled money matters

    when you were married.

Try to figure out your approximate monthly expenses.

Work out a budget.

Learn to balance your checkbook,
    even though you may feel totally inadequate at first.

Get help
    from friends already divorced,
    your lawyer,
    accountant,
    banker,
    real estate agent.

You need an efficient record-keeping
    system.

You may wish to establish credit
   in your own name.
Go to a major department store,
   or a credit card company.

Don't be surprised if you are turned down.
Strange, even if it was you who wrote
   the monthly checks while you were married.
Now that you are divorced, you are
   labeled a poor risk.

Don't give up.
Re-apply.
Find out if you are the object of
   "single discrimination."

And fight for your rights.

Eventually you will cope with your financial
   decisions,
and take this essential step toward controlling
   your own life.

Decisions About Children

Your children may say

"I hate you for being divorced."

"I want you to live together."

"I don't want you to leave."

"Please, please try again."

"Why are you doing this to *me*?"

You may resent hearing the
    same questions again and
    again.

But try to answer patiently and
    lovingly.
An understanding response will help the children
    accept what is happening in their lives.

You feel terrible
   when you know you are causing
   so much pain.

The marriage didn't work out.

But why should the children
   be hurt?

They are not to blame.

You have *not* forsaken your children.

They are better off in a single-parent home
   than in an unhappy atmosphere of
      tension and inconsistent values.

You provide the most nurturing home
   when you are happy with yourself.

Be truthful with them.
Tell your children how the divorce
    will change their immediate future.
Talk openly to them.

Evasions indicate your inability to
    handle the stressful situation.

Children suffer less from confusion
    and fantasies
    when they understand what is happening
    and know what to expect.
They will be better equipped
    to handle even the most difficult realities
    if they can depend on
    your being honest with them.

Your children may believe
   that they are responsible for the
   divorce.

Tell them again and again that they
   are not to blame.

You are unhappy with your ex
but not with them.

Many things in your marriage were not good,
   but the children represent what is best.

Children need to talk, not just
    to be talked to.

Real listening takes time.

Encourage them to share
    their feelings with you.

You can help by saying,
    "Tell me how you feel.
    I'll listen.
    I want to understand because
        I love you."

Don't rely completely on
    the spoken word.
The best approach is often nonverbal.

Hold them close.

Let them feel your warmth.

The key to helping your children
    is to make your own peace with the separation.

Decisions About Your Relatives

Keep your family informed about the
   developments of your divorce.
They have a right to know.
It may be hard for them to accept the fact
   that your marriage is over.

They are frightened.
They wonder what will happen to you
   and how it will affect them.

They may attempt to change your mind,
or ask that you live with them,
and try to take over your household.

Just remember:
No matter how much
you love them,
it is your life.

Parents have to allow their children
    to grow up.
Especially adult children.

Decisions About Friends

Your friends will learn of your separation,
    sooner or later.
The sooner they know, the better.

The way you tell them is important.
Perhaps you could confide in
a few close friends,
and suggest that they tell others.
You might write notes to a wider circle of
    acquaintances, including a change of address.
Or put a notice in your
    club or church or synagogue bulletin.

Find the most appropriate way for you,
    but let your friends know.
As you know, rumor breeds distortion.

Don't be surprised if some have already
expected it.
They may say,
"It's about time.
You should have done it years ago.
How did you manage to stay together
so long?"

Then the nosy questions:
  "What went wrong?
    Tell me.
    I won't tell anybody."

You need not answer in detail.
It's really not their concern.
You can simply say: "It didn't work out.
We decided to separate, that's all."

Some of your friends will abandon you.
They don't want to take sides.
Or they simply don't know what to say.
They may feel awkward in handling
   some situations now that you are single.

Social activities are geared for couples.
It's hard to know what to do with that
   extra person.

Like nine at a dinner party.

Now you know who your true friends are.
They understand and
   care,
   stay in touch,
   want to know how you are,
   and stand by your side.

Your definition of friendship has changed.
You have a clearer idea of
   the kind of friends you want
   and need.

Decisions About Changing "We" to "I"

You are used to "we."
   "What shall WE have for dinner?"
   "How shall WE spend our money?"
   "Where shall WE go for our vacation?"

A life of sharing becomes a habit
   not easy to break.

It's easy to find reasons to call your ex—
   about the children,
      the in-laws,
         finances,
            friends.
Any excuse will do.

Even fights are a way of prolonging
   the contact.

In the middle of a conversation
    with a friend,
you may blurt out,
"Have you seen my ex lately?"

You may still have a desire
    to learn what your ex is doing.

Maybe,
    there is a chance of
        putting the marriage
            back together again.

It's understandable,
part of the unwinding process.

When one moves out, you are
    separated *physically*.
But emotional separation is not such a
    quick process.
It takes a long time.

Very long.

Some contact may be necessary:
    if there are children,
    financial arrangements to be decided on;
    if you are living in the same community,
    belong to the same organizations.

God, it's hard meeting face to face.
Once intimate. Now strangers.

You feel again the stirrings of
    guilt, jealousy, pain, anger.
Even passion.

Perhaps you can set a goal—
to communicate when necessary, but
without falling apart.

When you talk with your ex,
try to concentrate on immediate problems.
Practice a businesslike approach.
Be brief.
Don't dwell on what went wrong
　　or who is to blame.

You are no longer part
    of a "we" relationship.
That's what divorce means.

Now it is "I."
Just you alone.
The marriage is over.

Divorce means saying
    Goodbye.

4 Rebuilding

Rebuilding

Divorce is a fact.

You are a single person,
   in charge of your own life.
There's only one name on the mailbox now.
Acceptance makes possible the
   open search for the resolution
   of your problems.

Facing reality is your first step
   in rebuilding a new existence.

"I AM DIVORCED."
"WE WILL NEVER LIVE TOGETHER AGAIN."

Can you say these words out loud?

Only when you confront the truth,
will you have the courage to
    endure pain.
Or the freedom to
    feel relief.

Talking Things Out

You may need a mourning period,
    a time to let go of your feelings.

An emotion that is denied expression
    is not destroyed.

It remains with you.
It may erupt at a less appropriate time.

To by-pass the emotional stress
    of grief
    is to prolong the agony
    and delay the cure.

It is better to explode in words
Than to take hasty action.

You may not like your thoughts.
They are unworthy of you, you think.

Nevertheless, they are there.

Verbalize your feelings
   of hostility and revenge.

Say the words.
Scream them,
   if you wish.
Even write them in your diary.
You may feel better.

Find a good listener.
A friend who will understand
   that hatred, jealousy, and guilt
   are authentic expressions of emotional separation.
A friend who will understand
   that grief never disappears
   when feelings are suppressed.

Acting out Feelings

Sometimes speech gets in the way.

Intellectualizing does not always help.

There is danger in over-analyzing
    emotions.

You may mask your real
    feelings with a camouflage
    of words.

There are other appropriate ways for
    expressing grief.

Are you angry?

Beat on a pillow as you shout your
  ex's name.
  Stamp and shout.
  Kick a ball.
  Run around the block.

You can use your energy profitably.
  Wash the car.
  Clean the windows.
  Straighten out the drawers.

Tears may be the best therapy
for emotional strain.

Weeping is a natural way to ease
anguish and release tension.

Let the tears flow without restraint.

Weep until the tears dilute
your pain and ease your grief.

You have a right to cry
    if you want to.

Tears are not evidence of weakness.

Crying expresses an inexpressible
    pain of separation,
of old memories, and
new responsibilities.

Everyone needs an outlet
    to discharge pent-up emotions.

You may seek escape
   from your torment through
     sleep,
     tranquilizers,
     alcohol,
     overwork,
     television,
     new conquests.

You are only delaying the grieving process.

There are no detours around the
   pangs of separation.

Express your emotions.

Act out your feelings.

Up From Grief—Slowly

First thoughts of working through grief
    are more theoretical than practical.

All kinds of possibilities are tossed
    around in your mind.

Some are born of wishful thinking.

Others are wildly unrealistic.

The road ahead is unfamiliar.

Acting on the first tentative
    plans can be dangerous.

Finding your way back into a
    meaningful existence,
is like navigating in
a metropolitan area without a road map.

Weigh matters as carefully as you can.

Panic causes one to think negatively.
    act rashly,
        draw hasty conclusions.

Don't rush into irreversible decisions like
   selling your house,
   changing your job,
   moving to another community.

The more familiar the routine and
   environment,
the more rapid may be your adjustment to
   altered circumstances.

Before making any major decisions,
seek professional advice,
   especially on business and legal matters.

At the eye of the hurricane
is a place of
calm.

You need patience
and time
to get your bearings.

Memories, Memories

You and your ex have divided your belongings.
You have sorted through
    many reminders of your life together.

There may be photographs of your honeymoon,
    of family fun,
    souvenirs from vacations,
    or gifts once chosen with great care
        and love.

Right now you may not want to see them,
    or even have them nearby.

They just evoke tears and sadness.

You may be tempted to destroy them.

Wait.
Don't get rid of them *quite* yet.
Put them away in a box.

Who knows?
You may wish to see them at a later time.

They are the chronicle of your past,
and could someday serve as
    a measure of how much you
    have grown and matured,
    not only in physical appearance
    but in your perspective.

You may not always wish to be sheltered
    from memories,
    tender and terrible,
    comforting and caustic.

Time, the Healer

You need time to convalesce.

Grief is a state of being.

It is a process.

There is no "normal time span"
  in which healing takes place.

Take as much time as you need.

Time is a staff on which
   you can rely.

Lean on it.

Give yourself the rest you need,
   to gather the strength to
   step forward again,
   into life.

Setbacks

You finally feel that you are
   on the right track.

The pain is not *so* intense.
At times you even enjoy yourself.
You are moving to recovery—
   at long last.
It's about time.

And then,
   then,
you find an old letter,
   see a couple walk hand in hand.

Most devastating of all,
you have an encounter with your ex.

Birthdays,
anniversaries, and
holidays
   are especially difficult.

Even a song,
   a book,
   a place,
can hurl you into despair.

Just when you were beginning to feel better;
when you thought you were out of the woods.

Setbacks are natural.
They're to be expected.

You survived pain before.
You will again.

But note:
This time the anguish is not so prolonged.
It passes more quickly.

You are learning to cope with suffering.

You are healing.

You *are* stronger.

Reorganization

In spite of setbacks and bad days,
you may be starting to look
    to the future with less anxiety.

You may be ready to make some
    plans
    to reorganize your life.

Where to begin?

Start with a checkup,
a complete physical examination.

If you are in poor health, you will not
    continue to heal,
    or grow stronger,
    and rebuild your life.

Begin to
eat properly,
sleep regular hours.

Exercise eases tension.

Begin by taking care of yourself.

If you don't, who will?

Routine chores
do not demand too much exertion
and concentration.

Like
restocking the cupboard,
making a dental appointment,
having the car repaired,
opening a new account.

As you begin to care for yourself,
you may find new sources of energy
and strength.

There are matters basic to your
survival that you *must* act on.

Look over your priorities.
What must be done as soon as possible?
What can be kept on the back burner?
Who can help you?
What are the possible solutions?

You may consider group-counseling sessions.
You could benefit from the experience
of others, and from their practical ideas
    about coping with problems
like finding someone to share house expenses,
handling the former in-laws,
combining the single life with
    child-rearing,
knowing what to do with a married
    person "on the make."

After you make decisions
    and act on them,
life begins to have meaning.

Life makes more sense.

Have a schedule for the day.

You may not always carry it out.

But have a plan.

You won't solve all the problems at once.
That's for sure.

It is also sure that no one but
you can reorder your life.

You hold the key to recovery.
Recovery starts when you
    begin to do things for yourself.

You already know that
    life involves risk.

The Risk of Going Out

A friend invites you over.
You don't want to go.
It's easier to stay home.

Try to go.

You feel strange.
Is everybody looking at you?
"How are you?" takes on
    a new meaning.

There is no safety in crowds.

After you circulate, there is no partner to
    come back to.
You feel like a fifth wheel.

Now that you're divorced,
you don't know what to say.

Your conversation can be
what you've always talked about:
  children,
  a new book,
  the latest political crisis.

Allow yourself to be drawn into a world
larger than your own pressing problems.

You may even enjoy yourself.
Pleasure is contagious.

Don't escape into loneliness.

Recluses don't recover.

And Having Fun Again

You need to rediscover that you
    can enjoy life.

Maybe go to
    an elegant restaurant,
    a football game,
    an evening at the opera.

Your ex may not have enjoyed what
you like to do.
Now you can concentrate on pleasing yourself.

Ask a friend to share your pleasure.

You also need to be alone,
to rest your body and your mind.

Spend a little time in a quiet place,
   a lovely, green park,
   a sunny country lane where you can walk,
   an empty church or synagogue.

A one-hour vacation can be helpful.

Your faith may help you
face and survive
moments of
   darkness and despair.

A little withdrawal and reflection
bring insights that strengthen you,
and allow you to return to the
world just a little different
from what you were.

You may uncover a kind of inner
tranquility that you never knew
existed.

Discovering New Skills

You did not want to,
but you *are* taking care of yourself.

Doing things you had never done before
    selling or buying a house,
    borrowing money,
    changing the bag on the vacuum cleaner,
    organizing a car pool,
    running the washing machine.

"I've never cooked a meal."
    You just broiled a steak and
      tossed a salad.

"I know nothing about cars."
    You just changed a flat tire,
      survived an encounter
        with a garage repairman.

You are alone and surviving,
discovering abilities that you never knew
you possessed.

Each success brings an inner satisfaction.
Self-confidence is starting to return.

You are becoming less dependent,
and more in control of your life.

Look at the calendar.

How many days have gone by
since you first separated?

You are not the same person.

There is a future for *you*.

Congratulate yourself.

Dating

In time you may want to date.

You may be afraid.

"Am I attractive,
    desirable,
    needed?"

"Will I be rejected?"

Again?

The dating scene is a real shock.
Especially after many years of being
part of a married couple.

You feel like a teenager all over again,
self-conscious and uncertain,
worried about what to wear,
with a nervous voice,
   and clammy hands.

Almost all the people
who go out after a divorce,
feel the same way—
   embarrassed,
   even humiliated,
   at being a beginner all over again.

The problem is—
where to find eligible people?

It is so hard to know how to re-enter
   an existence you thought you had outgrown.

Let your friends know that you
want to meet people.

They won't know that you are ready,
until you tell them.

Religious groups
and organizations like Parents Without Partners
now provide
support and friendship opportunitites
for single adults.

A New Dating Game

Dating has changed since
you were single.

Many dates are casual,
more like friendship
than courting for marriage.

Women often pay their own way.
Men may have custody of the children.
Both men and women
may have to find babysitters, and
   juggle complicated schedules.

Some singles want only an
evening of companionship.
Others may be working toward a
definite commitment.

Some people assume you want
a one night stand.

You could be hurt if your expectations
are different from your date's.

Honesty and frequent communication are
the best ways to avoid unnecessary
pain in the future.

Don't fantasize about marriage with
the first person who responds to you.

The excitement of a new attraction is heady.
You have been starved for appreciation.

Don't confuse novelty
    or gratitude with love.
Your intense feelings may be a way
of proving something to your ex.
  "I'll show you."
  "You're not the only fish in the sea."
  "See! I am desirable!"

Take your time about getting involved.
You may need to become a whole person,
   by *yourself*,
before you take up a *shared* life again.

Single? Yes
But Also a Person Like Everybody Else

Don't limit yourself to single groups.

You need contact with other kinds
of people,
in different kinds of associations.

Start with those who can share
your interests:
    dance group,
    sailing club,
    studying a language,
    yoga.

Then you will have something in common,
   something to talk about
   right from the beginning.
Something to give.

Being around single *and* married people
   will help you to explore and
   discover new possibilities for
   the future.

Other Kinds of Help

After a time, you may need a different
kind of support.

Occasionally a setback becomes very serious.

You might have trouble focusing your eyes.
Or you may sigh frequently and get dizzy.

Reliance on escapes—drugs, alcohol, sleep—
    may be more frequent.

You may even wonder if you want to
    go on living.

There is nothing wrong in asking for help from
   your physician,
   mental health clinic,
   social service organization,
   psychologic or psychiatric association.

There is *everything* wrong with suffering
   when help may be available.

Getting professional assistance is not
   an admission of weakness.
It is, in fact, a demonstration of your
   determination and courage.

You *want* to get better,
and
you *are doing* something about it.

A Ceremony for Divorce?

For many there is a value in rituals.
  "Ceremonials require each individual,
   however deep his or her grief or
   confusion, to reach out in a way that
   gives depth and meaning to the present."

—Margaret Mead

There are rites for momentous occasions:
  A ceremony for birth,
        the miracle of life;
  A ceremony for marriage,
        the consecration of love;
  A ceremony for death,
        the commemoration of memory.

A divorce ritual might help you to
    achieve a more positive ending of your marriage,
        balancing the cold brutality and psychic
        limbo of the courtroom;
    accept in a straightforward manner
        the severing of your life together;
    share with your children the knowledge that
        parental responsiblities continue;
    give your friends an opportunity
        to demonstrate their understanding
        and support.

The ceremony could take place
  in a home,
  a clergy member's study,
  or at a religious service.

Some divorce rituals have already
been published.

Ask a minister, rabbi, or friend
to help you create a meaningful ceremony.

You might begin the ceremony with *Shalom*.
It is a Hebrew word,
Meaning *welcome,*
   farewell,
   peace.

To everything there is a season, and
a time for every matter under heaven—
a time to be born, and a time to die,
a time to break down, and a time to build up,
a time to weep, and a time to laugh,
a time to cast away stones, and a
   time to gather stones together,
a time to embrace, and a time to
   refrain from embracing,
a time to keep, and a time to cast away.

—Ecclesiastes

There was a season and a time,
when you said "*Shalom.*"
You *entered* your marriage with vows
   of love and permanence.
The hopes and dreams of marital
happiness have perished.

The relationship is ended.

Now the "season and a time" have come to say
Shalom—farewell.

You publicly acknowledge that your
vows cannot be kept.
You will no longer live together.

You must face the future alone.

To remove part of the bitterness
and start a life apart, you
may promise
that you will not be vindictive,
but as forgiving as you can.

You may promise that even though
you had failed as husband and wife,
you will now attempt to succeed as father and mother.

You have "acted out" the crisis of separation.

The ceremony is a commitment
to a new kind of relationship.

"To everything there is a season and
A time for every matter under heaven."

May you go forward
to find
  Shalom, peace.

Symbolically, the wedding ring may be
  placed upon a different finger.

5 Becoming Whole Again

Becoming Whole Again

When the marriage ended, you did not
think you would survive.

The authors of this book
cannot know where you are now.

But we can say that others
have gone before you.
They have made the tormented trip from
    marriage to divorce,
    to the single life,
    and whatever lies beyond.

Others have found
that life does not end with divorce.

Doors open.
You gain the courage to walk through them.

People enter your life.
You make discoveries.

Gradually, a miracle takes place.
You begin to heal,
to become whole again.

But Yesterday Is Still with You

A complete person has
memories of the past,
as well as curiosity about
    the future.

Keep your integrity by honoring the past.

If you are making child-support payments,
make them
    a first priority.

If you do not have custody of the children,
    keep alive your relationship with them
    by regular visits,
       frequent phone calls, and letters.
Let them know you care.

If you have custody,
    allow your ex to see the children without a battle,
    without asking the youngsters to recount
       the happenings of each visit,
    without making them feel guilty for
       enjoying themselves with their other parent.

You may now be ready to take out
the mementos of your marriage,
and look at them with clear eyes,

There were some happy days.

It was not all bad.
Your ex had some good qualities.
Otherwise, you would not have married
    in the first place.

The good parts are
part of your yesterdays.

They are a part of you.

There were days of pain that *both* of you experienced.
You may even look at the part *you* played in breaking
    down the relationship,
and admit that you had some responsibility for the
    collapse of the marriage.

That takes real strength,
    real maturity.

You learn from the past,
when you can admit that you made mistakes.

You may even weep with relief
that you are able to be so honest.

Most of all, forgive yourself for your human
weakness,
your ignorance,
your moments of selfishness.

When you forgive yourself,
you will be all the more able
to begin a new relationship.

You will be able to forgive others.
You will be able to love,
in spite of weakness.

Other Moments of Truth

Divorce is one of those rare moments
when you ask,
    "Who am I really?"
    "What do I want out of life?"
    "What is the meaning of existence?"
Philosophers ask those questions,
But rarely do ordinary people
    search for the answers.

Divorce pushes you to the edge of a cliff,
You are forced to make a decision,
    to respond to life.

A New Face in the Mirror

Do you remember the face you
   saw in the mirror, just after your divorce?

Look again.
What do you see?

A person you are glad to be.
A person with a sense of self,
   relieved of pain,
     looking forward.

You can start over
   after a time;
you can begin a new career,
   go back to school,
   move to a new part of the country,
      someplace you have always wanted to live,
      but your ex wouldn't consider it;
   take up a new enthusiasm—
      hang-gliding,
      ballroom dancing,
      tennis,
      poetry.

You can try a new hairstyle;
   a new meal schedule.

WHATEVER YOU PLEASE.

From the death of a marriage
there is birth.

"Defeat may serve as well as victory
 To shake the soul and let the glory out.
 When the great oak is straining in the wind,
 The boughs drink in new beauty and the
    trunk
 Sends down a deeper root on the windward
    side.
 Only the soul that knows the mighty grief
 Can know the mighty rapture. Sorrows come
 To stretch out spaces in the heart for joy."

—Edwin Markham

You discover that
you don't need to be married to be complete.

There are many ways to find
   happiness, completeness.

Marriage is one way, not the only way.

You are beginning to care more about yourself,
than about the opinions of your ex
and others.

You were a half person.
Now you are filling in the other half.
You are becoming a whole person,
   perhaps for the first time.

If you had stayed married,
you might have grown.
But you didn't.
The divorce may not have been welcome;
yet it is an event
that stimulated new growth.

You are different now.

Gaining an ability to
face reality,
relate to others,
be independent,
resolve conflict,
make decisions,
let go of the past,
and live in the present.

You are experiencing life
in a context of new meanings.

Once you equated togetherness with happiness.
You thought that companionship, security,
lifelong physical closeness,
spiritual and emotional growth
were all to be had for the twist of a ring
and the breathing of a vow.

Now you can be single
　and like it.

"Divorce, I do not like you.
   Not at all.

"But I will learn to live with you.
   Now that you have intruded into my life.

"You are powerful.
   Your stormy winds have bruised
      and buffeted me.

"But you will never defeat me.

"I will face you, lean into you,
   storm back at you, and find my own strength.

"I will mend, and change, and grow,
   and reshape my life,
   Until one day,
   you will be a memory with which I can live
   and I will taste of joy again."